Kevin & Lisa

A little enticement to come and
visit us one day so we can repay
your amazing hospitality, thankyou
so much.

Pip Steve & Tom

TE ARAROA

For Hana,
and my parents Diane and John,
for opening my eyes to the hills.

First published in 2015 by New Holland Publishers (NZ) Ltd
Auckland • Sydney • London

www.newhollandpublishers.com

5/39 Woodside Avenue, Northcote, Auckland 0627, New Zealand
1/66 Gibbes Street, Chatswood, NSW 2067, Australia
The Chandlery, Unit 9, 50 Westminster Bridge Road,
London SE1 7QY, United Kingdom

Published with the assistance of Federated Mountain Clubs of New Zealand.

ISBN: 978 1 86966 436 7

Managing Director: David Cowie
Publisher: Christine Thomson
Editor: Anna Brett
Designer: Thomas Casey
Production Director: Olga Dementiev
Printer: Toppan Leefung Printing Ltd

A catalogue record for this book is available from
the National Library of New Zealand

10 9 8 7 6 5 4 3 2 1

TE ARAROA

Walking New Zealand's
3,000-kilometre trail

PHOTOGRAPHY **MARK WATSON**

Deep in the Hills

Once I thought the land I had loved and known
Lay curled in my utmost self; musing alone
In the quiet room I unfolded the folded sea,
Unlocked the forest and the lonely tree,
Hill and mountain valley beach and stone,
All these, I said, are here and exist in me.

But now I know it is I who exist in the land;
My inmost self is blown like a grain of sand
Along the windy beach, and is only free
To wander among the mountains, enter the tree,
To turn again a sea-worn stone in the hand,
Because these things exist outside of me.

O far from the quiet room my spirit fills
The familiar valleys, is folded deep in the hills.

—RUTH DALLAS

PAGE 1 Northern Richmond Range from Mount Starveall, Nelson/Marlborough.

PAGES 2–3 Sunrise, Ninety Mile Beach, Northland.

PAGES 4–5 Descending from Roses Saddle to the Arrow River, Motatapu Alpine Track, Otago.

PAGE 6 Northbound view of Kāpiti Island from the Paekakariki Escarpment Track, Wellington.

CONTENTS

FOREWORD

Chance encounters are a part of Te Araroa's charm. In March 2015 my family was down on Cheltenham Beach, Auckland, dipping the toes of my London-born grand-daughter into New Zealand coastal water for the first time. Along the beach came a guy with a light green pack, and a long easy stride. I suspected he'd be a Te Araroa walker. I stopped him.

Yes, he was walking the trail, he said. And he was photographing the trail for a book. I know how hard it is to walk a route as strenuous as Te Araroa, and to photograph as well, but I came away from that beach encounter knowing the guy would do his book. I had an inkling too, he might do something special. Some months later he asked me to write a foreword.

I'm thrilled with Mark's book. The photographs encompass the New Zealand iconography at Cape Reinga, the Central Plateau, the Southern Alps, and they do that well, but watch also what happens in between. A thoughtful consciousness glides into bush interiors and across landscapes that we haven't seen before. Occasionally the severity of the trail itself intrudes – a long beach trek maybe, or breaking trail in snow on high saddles – but what makes the collection so interesting is the alert gaze of a long-distance tramper, that may alight on something as simple as the transition between green farmland and old bush. Or, within the trail's wilder landscapes, may see its human figures diminished by scale and distance, yet by that reduction, enhanced. The trail's more subtle spirit moves in images like these, and it takes a superb photographer, but also one inured to the trail, to see it.

This is a thrilling book because Mark Watson, like the trail itself, has made the land new again.

—**Geoff Chapple**, founder, Te Araroa

INTRODUCTION

Every year from September to December more than 150 walkers shoulder packs and depart from Northland's isolated Cape Reinga, their sights set on a 3,000 kilometre journey south. Motivated, curious and perhaps daunted, these walkers will tackle a profoundly varied landscape as they traverse the two islands that make up the Te Araroa Trail. A land lying on the Pacific Rim of Fire, New Zealand is created by tectonic plate collision: our volcanoes, ranges and landforms are a consequence. This story of the landscape frames the Te Araroa experience.

Te Araroa starts with a mellow preamble along clifftops, scenic, windswept stretches of sand, past Cape Maria van Diemen and over headlands where a view south can sometimes be snatched. The fresh air, hardy plants and unique colour and form of the landscape usher the walker into a new world, away from traffic and work routines.

Then comes the first test: Ninety Mile Beach. Conditions largely dictate your experience, but camping in the sand, drinking swamp water, repetitious walking and blisters are common to most. With sand dunes to one side and the roaring ocean to the other, your view is channelled down the beach to a shimmering horizon. It can be blazingly hot, comfortable with a sea breeze or the wind stinging with sand particles. Some will love the walk and some will hate it. It's said that if you can survive the beach, you can handle anything else Te Araroa might throw at you.

Those who continue will be rewarded by the myriad experiences and challenges – both physical and mental – that the trail delivers. They'll be brought to their knees on the bad days, float over alpine passes on the good days and they'll be entranced by Te Araroa's pathway through New Zealand landscapes, towns and culture.

Generally, those tramping Te Araroa are a mixture of Kiwis, undertaking what could perhaps be seen as the ultimate rite-of-passage, and self-reliant overseas travellers looking for a challenging way to see New Zealand – some of whom are veterans of overseas long-distance tramps. Many Kiwis 'section tramp' Te Araroa, biting off a bit at a time, as few have the luxury of time and freedom from commitments to undertake the trail as a 'through-tramp'. Then there are the record-breakers, those walking the trail for a cause and people pursuing a new realm of life experience.

However it's tackled and for whatever reason, walkers will experience a unique view of New Zealand. It's a rigorous trek from tip to toe of a young country – the last significant islands on our planet to be peopled – that makes creative use of parks and forests, walkways, historic sites and the lie of the land to interconnect townships and points of interest, some well known, some obscure. If Te Araroa has one constant, it's change: New Zealand's subtropical north and colder south are latitudes apart, and reveal a varied geology and greatly divergent biota along the length of the islands – particularly noticeable by the many different kinds of forest encountered.

The form of the trail as we know it today is the result of the vision and determination of one man, Aucklander Geoff Chapple. An energetic author and journalist with a sparkle in his eye, Chapple took up where the government's New Zealand Walkway Commission, set up in 1975, had left off. As Chapple recounts in his book, *Te Araroa – The New Zealand Trail, One Man Walks His Dream*, Bob Ussher of the Alpine Sports Club initially proposed the idea of a national trail in 1967. Federated Mountains Clubs endorsed the concept and supported a plan, which went to government. The formation of the Walkway Commission, with a mandate to establish walkways, was successful in creating short trails; over 130 of them in 12 years, but the overall vision for a single trail faltered in the face of opposition from landowners. The Walkway Commission ceased in 1987, with the newly formed Department of Conservation absorbing its role, but failing to make progress with the trail. In 1994 a *Sunday Star* article by Chapple reactivated the idea and captured the public imagination. The formation of the Te Araroa Trust followed in the same year. 1998 saw Chapple pioneer a possible route in the North Island, gauging landowner response, building relationships and raising the profile of the trail. A walk of the South Island followed in 2002 and the trail was born.

The Te Araroa Trail

North Island through-tramper Holger Horner among the mountain beech of Dora Ridge, near Te Matawai Hut. Tararua Range.

Walking is as natural – and essential – to mankind as eating, sleeping and reproducing. Overnight recreational walking takes place the world over, on a mixture of historic routes and trails established for the purpose. But there are few true long distance (3,000 km-plus) walking trails that cross a great swathe of country. One of the most venerable is the Appalachian Trail (AT) in the eastern USA. Completed in 1937 and covering 3,500 km, the trail receives about 1,800–2,000 through-hikers annually, with an estimated one-in-four completing the walk. The western USA Pacific Crest Trail (PCT) traces a path from Mexico to Canada for 4,265 km and the less well-known Continental Divide Trail clocks in over 5,000 km. Long distance trails are planned in Japan, Canada and Italy. Through-trampers embarking on Te Araroa during the 2014/2015 season (including those doing single islands) reportedly numbered around 200. The popularity of long distance through-hiking has spawned a culture of lightweight travel and even its own lexicon: with terms like 'trail magic' and 'trail angels' (terms for the spirit of volunteerism and gifting), 'zero' (a rest day) and 'SOBO/NOBO' (southbound/northbound).

Something that sets the Te Araroa Trail apart from its American cousins is its variety. Where the AT and PCT are essentially wilderness trails, occasionally interrupted by towns and with services a hitch-hike away, Te Araroa's North Island leg frequently passes through towns – and two big cities – as it connects short, one- to four-day, tramping sections. It utilises urban walkways, farm tracks, beaches, roads and regional parks as well as longer tracks in forest and national parks. This creates a journey that gives opportunity for historic, cultural and social insights and highlights the differences between each region. The South Island, by contrast, comprises a series of remoter tramps interspersed with small towns. One way of comparing the two islands is to consider that in the North Island I usually kept my wallet in my pocket, but in the South Island it was buried in my pack and forgotten about for up to eight days at a time.

Starveall Hut, one of many classic ex-deer culler's huts on the Richmond Alpine Track, captured in bright moonlight.

Lake Wakatipu and Cecil Peak, Queenstown.

In mid January 2015 I set out from Cape Reinga on a hot summer's day to walk and photograph the Te Araroa Trail in its entirety. I had the company of my partner, Hana, for the first few days and she joined me intermittently over the remaining 147 walking days of my journey. The majority of the trail I walked alone – content with a solo journey focused on waking in the dark daily in the hope of finding interesting light and subjects as I moved across the country, and aiming to be somewhere compelling to shoot towards the end of the day. For five months and 20 days my existence revolved around walking, making photographs, eating, reading and sleeping. It was one of the best experiences of my life.

I have tramped regularly since my pre-teen years and have visited most New Zealand parks. I'm no stranger to sustained journeys either; in 2011, I cycled 13,000 km from the Tibetan Plateau to Indonesia through seven South East Asian countries. I wanted to find out for myself what the Te Araroa Trail entailed; to photograph the view of New Zealand that it presents. Telling not only the story of the landscape of the Te Araroa Trail; invoking a sense of place, but also creating a narrative of my own through-tramp experience; illustrating the changing seasons and conditions. I hope there is an intimacy and honesty in the images; they're an expression of the 'here and now' of walking the trail rather than a presentation of the most picturesque sections of the trail in the nicest light. Another of my aims was to inspire others to go and appreciate the fulfillment and simplicity that comes from crossing the land on foot.

During my scouting years, as a teenager, a fellow scout's father – himself an enthusiastic tramper and black and white photographer – used to come to our evenings and give slide shows of his experiences walking in New Zealand and Australia. One evening he concluded his show by saying that he'd been tramping for many years before he 'noticed that the trees had tops'. This was his way of saying: be observant, witness nature both in its subtlety and its rawness and take an interest in your surroundings. This book is about what's at the top of the trees.

NORTHLAND

NORTHLAND
Cape Reinga–Mangawhai

The real voyage of discovery consists
not in seeking new landscapes,
but in having new eyes.
—MARCEL PROUST

To Māori Cape Reinga is known as Te Rerenga Wairua, The Leaping-off Place of the Spirits. Mythology dictates that this wind-buffeted promontory; embraced by the temperate waters of the Tasman Sea to its west, and the Pacific Ocean to the east, is where the spirits of the dead enter the underworld to begin their long journey to their traditional homeland, Hawaiki via the Te Ara Wairua (The Spirit's Pathway).

So too is it the origin of journey for this trek south. Descending an airy cliff edge path from the lighthouse, the trail crosses a web of sand stretching towards the bony knuckles of Herangi Hill and Cape Maria van Diemen. Bays and breezy headlands follow on the pleasant walk to the start of Ninety Mile Beach. The extreme tips of any country are often its remotest and this isolated location is no different. For most Te Araroa walkers, the walk to the tiny town of Ahipara will take three to four days and there is little in the way of resupply en-route. Water is scarce and the environment can be challenging.

Beyond Ahipara the trail enters the first of many verdant Northland forests; remnants on the margins of farmland that invoke a frontier feel to the landscape. The trail emerges on the east coast at Kerikeri, one of New Zealand's oldest towns. Beaches, bush, rural communities, Kiwi holiday haunts and historic sites define much of the walk through Northland and it's fitting that Te Araroa should start in the region that was the genesis of New Zealand as a nation.

PREVIOUS PAGES Cape Reinga lighthouse and beyond, the merging waters of the Tasman Sea and Pacific Ocean. Starting point for the Te Araroa Trail.

OPPOSITE A cliff-top pathway, the first steps of Te Araroa, heads towards Te Werahi Beach and Cape Maria van Diemen.

ABOVE Cape Reinga lighthouse at dawn.

OPPOSITE Twilight Beach/Te Paengarehia, popular as a first overnight stop for many trampers.

ABOVE The apparently endless expanse of Ninety Mile Beach/Te Oneroa-a-Tōhē stretches away from Scott Point. Matapia Island sits just offshore.

OPPOSITE The view north over the Te Paki sand dunes towards Scott Point.

OPPOSITE Early morning, walking down Ninety Mile Beach.

LEFT King tides pound Te Wakatehaua Island, The Bluff, Ninety Mile Beach.

RIGHT Wairoa Stream and Ahipara Peak, Ahipara. The view of this distinctive peak signalling an end to the remoteness of Ninety Mile Beach.

LEFT Kauri tree trunk and astelias. A stand of these mighty, and endangered, conifers is a highlight of the Herekino Forest walk.

TOP RIGHT Houses and Ahipara Peak, an historic pa site, Ahipara.

BOTTOM RIGHT Makene Road, Mangamuka.

Church alongside State Highway One, Mangamuka.

OPPOSITE Totara tree – a common sight throughout Northland, Mangamuka.

ABOVE Mangapukahukahu Stream, followed by the Te Araroa Trail through the Omahuta Forest.

OPPOSITE Young kauri, Pukatea Ridge, Puketi Forest.
TOP LEFT TO RIGHT Waiare Road, Puketi; farm tracks, Puketotara Farm, Kerikeri.
BOTTOM LEFT TO RIGHT Rainbow Falls, Kerikeri River Track; puriri tree and regenerating bush, Kerikeri River Track; silver tree fern and supplejack, Kerikeri River Track.

TOP LEFT Stone Store, New Zealand's oldest stone bulding. Kerikeri.

TOP RIGHT Mission House, Kerikeri. New Zealand's oldest surviving building, completed in 1882.

BOTTOM LEFT Te Whare Rūnanga (the House of Assembly), Waitangi Treaty Grounds, Waitangi.

BOTTOM RIGHT Estuary bridge, Waitangi.

OPPOSITE Paihia township.

OPPOSITE Ancient log weir, Papakauri Stream. The stream bed itself providing Te Araroa's route into Russell Forest.

LEFT Rural home and farmland, Mokau.

RIGHT Ōtetau Reti marae, Punaruku.

OPPOSITE Northbound view along the Whananaki Footbridge, claimed to be the longest in the Southern Hemisphere.
ABOVE Sandy Bay, Whananaki Coastal Walk.

Pohutukawa trees, Sandy Bay, Whananaki Coastal Walk.

Festival signage alongside road walk out of Ngunguru.

OPPOSITE Horahora River estuary, Horahora.
ABOVE Pataua River footbridge, Pataua.

OPPOSITE Awahoa Bay and the volcanic remnant islands of the Poor Knights from Kauri Mountain.

LEFT Crossing volcanic boulders on Ocean Beach. Bream Head in background.

RIGHT Remains of WWII naval radar installation and Hen and Chickens Islands, Bream Head Track.

LEFT Section tramper Hana Black checks out an epiphyte-draped puriri tree, Bream Head Track.

RIGHT Natural jetty formed by an andesitic dike, Taurikura Bay, Whangarei Harbour.

Marsden Point Oil Refinery and Reotahi Bay homes from Mount Aubrey. Te Araroa crosses the harbour here to continue along the coastline to distant hills.

OPPOSITE Manaia and Bream Head (distant centre) from Mount Aubrey.

TOP LEFT Township of Waipu, settled by Scottish Highlanders in the 1850s.

TOP RIGHT Cliff edge trail and Mangawhai Heads, Mangawhai Walkway.

BOTTOM LEFT Pohutukawa trees, Mangawhai Walkway.

BOTTOM RIGHT Coastline, Mangawhai Walkway.

AUCKLAND

AUCKLAND
Mangawhai–Mercer

hitched up my bundle
went down the street
long way to go
walking on my feet
—FROM *WALKING ON MY FEET*, A.R.D. FAIRBURN

Te Araroa's journey from the craggy coastline of Mangawhai to Mercer is one of contrast: from the crunch of shells beneath the feet on peaceful beaches to the hum of traffic in Auckland City. Thankfully, it's a gradual change, as the rural quiet of Northland gives way to bigger roads and increasing population density. The offshore bird sanctuary of Little Barrier Island/Hauturu becomes a gauge of progress for the walk along the coast and into the hills of Omaha Forest. Tamahunga (437 m), provides views to the Sky Tower; a reminder that New Zealand's biggest city draws close.

The quaint township of Puhoi, settled by Bohemians in the 1860s, has an intact sense of history. From here the route takes to the river for a return to the coast at Wenderholm Regional Park; the trail south now defined by steep headlands, estuaries and the gentle cone of Rangitoto Island.

New Zealand's first capital, Auckland is the centre of commerce for New Zealand and Te Araroa is unique for a long distance trail; weaving right through its centre and allowing all of the opportunities of a big city. The hefty dynamics of volcanism are responsible for much of Auckland's topography and as the trail continues it crosses the cones of Mount Eden/Maungawhau and One Tree Hill/Maungakiekie – wonderful vantage points to take in the scope and complexity of Auckland City, spread as it is over a narrow isthmus. The first steps into the Hunua Range beyond the city come as a relief after traversing over 70 km of road and footpath in this urban excursion.

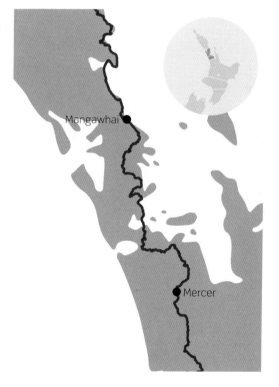

PREVIOUS PAGES Auckland City framed beyond the lip of Mount Eden/Maungawhau's volcanic crater. Coast to Coast Walkway.

OPPOSITE Sandstone tidal terraces at Long Bay Regional Park usher the walker towards Torbay, the first of Auckland's North Shore suburbs.

LEFT Taranga Island and Sail Rock viewed through cove at Eyre Point.

RIGHT Northern rata and host tree among nikau and broadleaf forest, Omaha Forest.

Whangateau Harbour from Omaha Forest.

TOP LEFT Nikau trunk, Dome Forest.

TOP RIGHT Streamlands Swamp Road, Streamlands.

BOTTOM LEFT Kourawhero Hall, Woodcocks Road, Kourawhero.

BOTTOM RIGHT Remnant puriri and nikau forest, Dunns Bush. Gifted to the QEII National Trust by the Dunn Family in 1994.

TOP LEFT A welcome sight, the Puhoi Pub and Hotel. A small valley township, Puhoi was settled by Bohemians in the 1860s.

TOP RIGHT Church and hall, Puhoi.

BOTTOM LEFT A kayak transition down the Puhoi River avoids State Highway 17, en route to Wenderholm Regional Park.

BOTTOM RIGHT Headlands and Puhoi River mouth, Wenderholm Regional Park.

TOP LEFT Pohutukawa tree at Grannys Bay, Long Bay Regional Park.

TOP RIGHT Long Bay Regional Park and Torbay, the first of Auckland's North Shore suburbs. The view of Rangitoto Island beyond will be a constant companion for the walk south.

BOTTOM LEFT Rangitoto Island and sandstone tidal flats, Red Bluff, Campbells Bay.

BOTTOM RIGHT WWII gun emplacements on North Head/Maungauika, Devonport.

Auckland City and Devonport from North Head/Maungauika.

LEFT An interior view of Victoria Street and Auckland's Sky Tower.

TOP RIGHT Pohutukawa trees, Auckland Domain/Pukekawa.

BOTTOM RIGHT One Tree Hill/Maungakiekie, decorated with its obelisk; a presumptuous 'memorial' to Māori, Coast to Coast Walkway.

Ambury Regional Park, Puketutu Island and Manakau Harbour, an important migratory bird habitat, from Mangere Mountain.

TOP LEFT Te Araroa takes a suburban route through Wiri, Manurewa, Northbound view.

TOP RIGHT Road junction, Alfriston.

BOTTOM LEFT Takeaway store and main street, Clevedon.

BOTTOM RIGHT Kimptons Track and Clevedon Reserve form a backdrop behind a rural road, Clevedon.

OPPOSITE Wairoa Dam, part of Auckland's water supply, Hunua Ranges.

Sunrise on Lyons Road, Mangatawhiri.

An early morning Brocken (mist) bow touches down on the Mangatawhiri River Track stopbank.

WAIKATO/KING COUNTRY

WAIKATO/KING COUNTRY
Mercer–Tongariro National Park

Waikato-taniwha-rau   *Waikato of a hundred taniwha*
He piko, he taniwha   *At every bend a taniwha can be found.*
He piko, he taniwha.
—MĀORI PROVERB

The mighty Waikato River – New Zealand's longest – defines much of the journey through the Waikato. It's a land shaped by eruptions and etched both by the river and with the history of people; ancient pa sites, redoubts and memorials to the New Zealand wars dot the landscape. To Māori, the Waikato is an ancestor with whom they maintain a deeply spiritual connection. Many marae are located on its banks, notably, Tūrangawaewae at Ngāruawāhia; headquarters of Te Kīngitanga, the Māori King Movement.

Flat travel along the Waikato's bank provides a respite from hills until the steeply lifted Hakarimata Range is reached. Clothed with rich broadleaf podocarp forest, this bumpy range is one of New Zealand's oldest walkways. Beyond Hamilton the broken basaltic cones of Pirongia Mountain dominate the skyline. An island of bush amid farmed hill country, this volcano indicates a transition zone between warm northern kauri forest and southern forests, and a variety of trees cover its slopes. Blanched rock outcrops and a mysterious topography typify the limestone landscape either side of Pirongia. As the trail gains elevation climbing Mangaokewa Stream towards the volcanic plateau, it nudges into pumice and ignimbrite country – a landscape wrought by eruptions from the site of Lake Taupo.

At Pureora, there is one of the largest remaining tracts of native forest in the North Island; ancient podocarp species and a rich rainforest understorey swallow you in world of green. From the summit of Mount Pureora New Zealand's biggest lake can be seen, the distinctive mountains of Tongariro National Park shape the horizon and the folded watershed of the Whanganui River – the journey onwards from the volcanoes – stretches away.

PREVIOUS PAGES A northbound view over pockets of native bush towards Pirongia Mountain, from the Mahoe Forest Track.

OPPOSITE Mist shrouds a stand of kahikatea trees at dawn, north west of Te Kuiti.

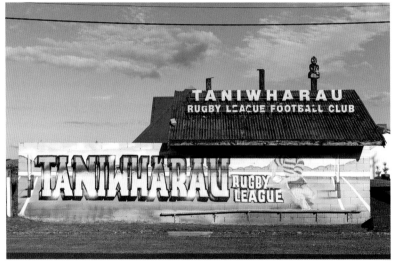

TOP LEFT Headstones and unnamed British graves at Rangiriri, site of the decisive battle of the Waikato War.

TOP RIGHT The Waikato River at Huntly with Hakarimata Range in the distance.

BOTTOM LEFT State house, West Huntly.

BOTTOM RIGHT Taniwharau rugby club building, West Huntly.

Northbound view from the Hakarimata Range. Huntly and the Huntly Power Station flank the Waikato River.

Broadleaf forest, Hakarimata Range, one of New Zealand's oldest walkways.

Confluence of the Waikato and Waipa Rivers below the Hakarimata Range, Ngaruawahia.

LEFT Historic Waipa Hotel, Ngaruawahia.

RIGHT Tūrangawaewae House, Ngaruawahia. Built as a parliament house for the Kīngitanga (King movement) and opened in 1919.

LEFT Fairfield Bridge and Waikato River from the Hamilton City River Walk.

RIGHT After departing the Waikato River, Te Araroa takes a route through central Hamilton, then through its western suburbs.

TOP LEFT Karst country forms hillocks of limestone, Kapamahunga Walkway.
BOTTOM LEFT Noel Sanford boardwalk, Hihikiwi Track, Pirongia Mountain.
RIGHT Dracophyllum, Hihikiwi Track, Pirongia Mountain.
OPPOSITE Sunrise over the bush-covered basalt summits of Pirongia Mountain.

Northbound view of Pirongia West Road and Pirongia Mountain bush fringe.

View north across rolling hill country to Kakepuku from Mahoe Forest Track.

TOP LEFT View west down Pirorua Stream, from Mahoe Forest Track.

TOP RIGHT Silver tree fern/punga, Mahoe Forest Track.

BOTTOM LEFT Rugby field, Waitomo.

BOTTOM RIGHT Kahikatea grove, Pehitawa Forest – one of the finest remaining groves in the North Island.

Old shop houses, Te Kuiti; the only sizable resupply town between Hamilton and Taumarunui.

LEFT Parataniwha nettle and tawa forest, Mangaokewa Reserve Track.

RIGHT Mangaokewa Stream forms a border between substantial old growth native forest on the east side and farmland on the west.

Totara trees and farmland, Upper Mangaokewa Valley.

LEFT Lichen on fencepost, Mangaokewa North Road.

TOP RIGHT Derelict barn, Mangaokewa North Road.

BOTTOM RIGHT Te Hape Marae, Bennydale.

OPPOSITE Volcanic country, shaped by eruptions from the site of Lake Taupo, rolls towards the peak of Pureora.

LEFT Young kahikatea trees on farmland, near Tiroa.

RIGHT Freshly felled pine trees and old growth podocarp forest, Timber Trail, Pureora Forest.

OPPOSITE The richly bush covered hills of Pureora Forest stretch towards Lake Taupo and the Central North Island volcanoes from the summit of Pureora.

OPPOSITE Mount Taranaki and Whanganui River catchment south west of Pureora.

TOP LEFT Track junction, Pureora Forest.

TOP CENTRE AND RIGHT Kidney fern growing thickly on a spur (centre); the curly upper limbs of a montane totara (right), Hauhungaroa Range.

BOTTOM LEFT Tree fuschia/kotukutuku with its distinctive red, ribbony bark. Pureora Forest.

BOTTOM RIGHT Trunk of a large montane totara tree, Hauhungaroa Range.

OPPOSITE Derelict farmhouse and flat-topped Hikurangi (771 m), Ngakonui, en route to Taumarunui.

LEFT Whare entrance-styled gateway, Ngakonui–Ongarue Road.

RIGHT Taranaki Daily News building, Taumarunui.

LEFT Basalt boulder and Whakapapa River, Owhango. Start of the 42 Traverse Track.

TOP RIGHT North Island through-trampers Holger Horner and Barry Savage examine the convoluted landscape of the 42 Traverse.

BOTTOM RIGHT Te Pōrere Redoubt, in 1869 the site of the last major battle of the New Zealand Wars. Mount Tongariro cloud capped in the distance.

OPPOSITE Mounts Tongariro and Ngauruhoe from Access Road No. 3, Central Plateau.

WHANGANUI

WHANGANUI
Tongariro National Park—Bulls

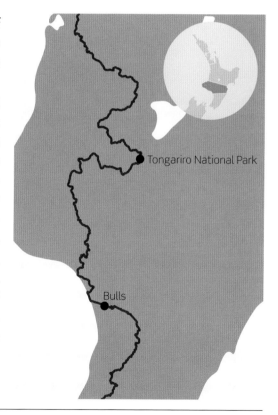

Te Araroa's route is defined by the Pacific Ring of Fire; the earth building processes of which have formed the ranges and volcanoes of New Zealand. The Tongariro Alpine Crossing, with a high point of 1,868 m at Red Crater is the North Island zenith of the walker's experience of this aspect of the landscape.

Between the volcanoes of Tongariro and Ngauruhoe is a barren but vibrant world of ochre, orange and grey and hardy alpine plants; then the beech forest and tussock grasslands of Mount Ruapehu. A more modified landscape follows as the trail heads east from National Park to meet the Whanganui River at Whakahoro. For Māori the Whanganui River was central to life in the bush; a passage to the interior and in pre-European times it was a densely populated region. For walkers the river is a conduit for a journey from the high plateau of the volcanoes to the coast; a transition from a desert-like environment, through rainforest – following strands of history – to the Tasman Sea.

Between Whakahoro and the mythical Bridge to Nowhere the trail tells a story of a landscape grappled with, and ultimately abandoned, by settlers. For Māori every bend and rapid of the Whanganui has a guardian, or kaitiaki, who maintains the life force of that stretch of the river and it should be with respect that walkers enter the river when the trail ceases at Mangapurua Landing. Onwards, the choice is canoe or jet boat, at least as far as the tiny settlement of Pipiriki and for some, further – towards Whanganui city. Wherever walking continues, it's with a sense of completeness that you reach the quiet coastal settlement of Koitiata, south of Whanganui.

PREVIOUS PAGES The Whanganui River cuts a path though soft papa (mudstone) hills at Pungarehu. Mount Ruapehu, close to the river's source, is visible at top right.

OPPOSITE Fishers Track leads into steep hills beyond National Park.

OPPOSITE Steam issues from vents at the Emerald Lakes at sunrise, Tongariro Alpine Crossing.

ABOVE The author taking in the view of South Crater and Mount Ngauruhoe, Tongariro Alpine Crossing.

Lava, some from eruptions within the last 60 years, shapes the landscape of the Mangatepopo Valley beneath Mount Ngauruhoe and Pukekaikiore.

TOP LEFT Mountain cabbage tree/toii on the Whakapapaiti Valley Track, Tongariro National Park.

BOTTOM LEFT Tussock and fern covered bench, Whakapapaiti Valley, Mount Ruapehu.

RIGHT Mangahuia Stream, Tongariro National Park.

LEFT An autumn sunrise directly over the summit of Mount Ngauruhoe.

RIGHT The gentle forms of Mounts Ngauruhoe and Ruapehu backdrop State Highway Four at National Park.

LEFT Oio Road, en route to Whakahoro.

TOP RIGHT The tiny settlement of Whakahoro, entry point for the Mangapurua–Kaiwhakauka Track.

BOTTOM RIGHT An old school house, restored and converted into a Department of Conservation bunkroom at Whakahoro.

OPPOSITE Battleship Bluff and Mangapurua Stream, Mangapurua Track.

TOP LEFT Long abandoned automobile on the Mangapurua–Kaiwhakauka Track.

BOTTOM LEFT Relaxing at Johnsons Campsite, Mangapurua Track.

RIGHT Bridge to Nowhere, Mangapurua Valley. Built in 1936, but scarcely utilised, as the government and the settlers it was constructed for abandoned the rugged land soon after its completion.

TOP LEFT Like a memorial cross, a sign indicates the ownership surnames of land allocated to, and subsequently abandoned by, servicemen returning from WWI, Mangapurua Track.

BOTTOM LEFT Canoe transition down the Whanganui River.

RIGHT St Joseph's Church, Jerusalem.

TOP LEFT   The quiet, narrow road out of Pipiriki.

TOP RIGHT   Whanganui River and flood-deposited tree trunks.

BOTTOM LEFT   Ranana Marae, Whanganui River.

BOTTOM RIGHT   Village of Jerusalem and Whanganui River.

ABOVE Entering Whanganui City alongside the Whanganui River.

OPPOSITE Driftwood and beach at sunrise, Koitiata.

LEFT Marram and pingao grass covers sand dunes south of Koitiata, with the Tararua Range dark on the distant horizon.

RIGHT Farm buildings, Raumai Road, Bulls.

Rangatikei Tavern, Bulls.

MANAWATU/
WELLINGTON

MANAWATU/WELLINGTON
Bulls–Island Bay

Te tāpaepae o te rangi.
See there, to the place
where the sky reaches down.
—MĀORI PROVERB

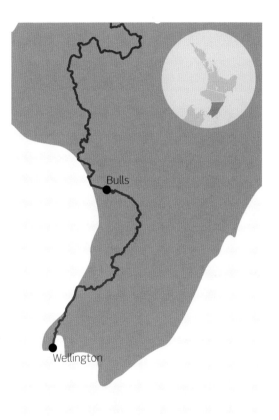

A symphony must have its meandering quiet to give pause and call attention to its apogee. Te Araroa has its own mixture of the mundane and the magnificent and the mostly flat trek from the coast, through Bulls and onwards to the foothills serves as a transition before the challenge and scenery of the Tararua Range – a North Island highlight.

The mellow farming country of the Manawatu Plain is framed by Mount Ruapehu to the north and the Ruahine and Tararua Ranges to the east. Ruapehu's distant massif gives a satisfying sense of country traversed; but distant bush-clad and golden tussock topped ridges beckon. The rural towns of Fielding – quaint and orderly, as if from an Enid Blyton story – and Palmerston North provide a chance to resupply.

Young mountains, steeply uplifted, the Tararuas have the potential to challenge the hardiest tramper. The trail's highpoint, Mount Crawford, is a modest 1,462 m but strong winds and rain are commonplace in a range so proximate to the Cook Strait. It is this high rainfall that creates the jungle-like environment of the western side of the range; dripping ferns and tangled bush envelop the tramper on the climb to Pukematawai. A distinctive feature of these ranges is the stunted, amorphous form of the moss-clad mountain beech that shelters the steep upper slopes and ridges.

The Kapiti Coast provides a pleasant entry to the outskirts of Wellington with Paekakariki Escarpment giving an eagle's eyrie view of the hills and mountains to the south. More variety follows as Colonial Knob, Mount Kaukau and some of Wellington's oldest suburbs guide you on a route to the rocky south coast and the North Island journey's end.

PREVIOUS PAGES From Paekakariki Escarpment Track, the view south to Pukerua Bay and the South Island beyond heralds the closing days of the North Island leg of Te Araroa.

OPPOSITE Wind farms and rolling farming country south west of Colonial Knob, Porirua.

OPPOSITE Mount Ruapehu stands proud beyond the Rangitikei River and Manawatu Plain, just outside Bulls.

LEFT Historic Glaxo building, origin of the GlaxoSmithKlein pharmaceutical company, Bunnythorpe.

RIGHT Manawatu River and Fitzherbert Bridge, Palmerston North.

LEFT Te Araroa's entry point to the Tararua Range at Poads Road. A long climb through bush to Waiopehu Hut follows.

RIGHT Ralph Wood's grave, Twin Peak. Ralph died of exposure during a powerful 1936 storm that destroyed huts and bush in much of the western Tararuas.

OPPOSITE Looking west to Te Matawai Hut from the climb to Pukematawai. Twin Peak, traversed by the trail, and the coast are beyond.

LEFT Typical stunted, moss-clad mountain beech on Tararua Main Range.

TOP RIGHT North Island through-trampers Barry Savage and Holger Horner resting at Dracophyllum Hut, Tararua Range.

BOTTOM RIGHT Departing Nichols Hut in stormy weather, Tararua Main Range.

TOP LEFT Beech forest with crown fern, tree fern and horopito understorey, Otaki River.

BOTTOM LEFT Beech forest alongside the Otaki River, near Waitewaiwai Hut.

RIGHT Swingbridge over the Otaki River.

TOP LEFT Kāpiti Island and Paraparaumu housing from Waikanae River estuary.

TOP RIGHT Regenerating broadleaf forest on Colonial Knob Walkway.

BOTTOM LEFT Pukerua Bay beach and Kāpiti Island.

BOTTOM RIGHT Te Araroa's pathway through the suburbs of Mana and Paremata alongside Porirua Harbour.

Grassy hillsides and open views en route to Ohariu Valley from Colonial Knob Walkway.

OPPOSITE Central Wellington, early evening, City to Sea Walkway.

LEFT Aro Street, in one of Wellington's more characterful suburbs, Te Aro, City to Sea Walkway.

RIGHT Wellington's suburbs Berhampore and Newtown, City to Sea Walkway. Mount Victoria is the prominent high point at left, while the Tararua Range crowns the centre horizon.

ABOVE Island Bay, terminus of Te Araroa in the North Island. Wellington Harbour and Rimutaka Range in the background.

OPPOSITE Homes, Island Bay, Wellington.

NELSON/ MARLBOROUGH

NELSON/MARLBOROUGH
Ship Cove–Boyle River

But if you stand alone in a trackless glen, hearing no sound save the wood pigeons up high … or a tui picking out his notes from an unseen branch, the twilight seems to creep almost audibly among the thickets, and the forest reveals itself as something that is not ours, something that has never belonged even to the Maori, but has known centuries of an undisturbed stillness...
—FROM *THE DEEPENING STREAM*, MONTE HOLCROFT [1940]

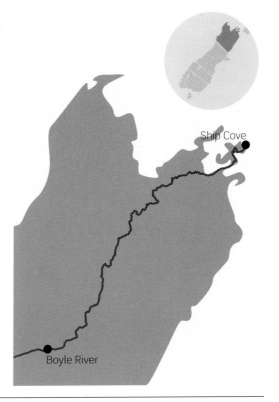

A sunken landscape of bushy ridges, incised by coves and lapped by sheltered waters sets the scene for the walk south from the top of Te Wai Pounamu. What better place to make landfall and take first steps onto the South Island than at the same place Captain James Cook and his intrepid crew anchored the Endeavour in 1770, while they replenished the ship's supplies.

Though hilly, the broad path of the Queen Charlotte Track makes for quick travel and coupled with Marlborough's mild climate the sounds provide an amiable warm up for hillier tramping beyond. Linkwater and Havelock provide the option to resupply and a change from the bush before the Richmond Range is entered past Pelorus Bridge. This sustained section – with regular huts – is a highlight, tackling a mixture of river valleys, the trail's highest South Island summit, bush and tussock ridges and the geological anomaly of the Red Hills ultramafic zone.

Postcard perfect, Lake Rotoiti is the entry point for Nelson Lakes National Park and the feast of alpine scenery that unfolds on the tramp to Blue Lake, among the moraines of the upper Sabine Valley. The clearest known freshwater lake in the world, Blue Lake is also the gateway to Waiau Pass, the second highest pass of Te Araroa. The craggy southern side is probably the trickiest terrain of Te Araroa as the trail descends to meet the Waiau River. Beyond, one of the biggest contrasts of the walk is revealed, as the trail departs native forest and enters scree streaked open valleys. Pockets of remnant beech follow as the St James Walkway is followed to the highway.

PREVIOUS PAGES Sunrise over the northern Richmond Range from Mount Starveall. The large swathes of flattened beech trees were blown over in a severe storm.

OPPOSITE Landslide material that blocked the Sabine River, forming Lake Constance, makes a great spot to boulder hop and check out the view towards Waiau Pass.

Resolution Bay, Queen Charlotte Track, named for its use as an anchorage by one of Captain Cook's ships.

LEFT Mussels along shoreline of Schoolhouse Bay, one of the Queen Charlotte track's finest camping bays.

TOP RIGHT Once dry valleys, now a landscape of sounds, Marlborough's many headlands make for scenic tramping.

BOTTOM RIGHT Manuka grove, typical of the regenerating bush along much of the Queen Charlotte Track.

LEFT Endeavour Inlet, Queen Charlotte Track.

RIGHT Occasional, and spectacular, stands of remnant beech forest make the Queen Charlotte Track a varied walk.

LEFT Nesting cormorant, Mahakipawa Arm, Havelock.

RIGHT A logging truck crosses the Pelorus River at Pelorus Bridge; from here the trail's route turns into the ranges.

TOP LEFT Section tramper Pete Griffin in the rich red beech forest of the Pelorus River Track.

TOP RIGHT Crossing swingbridge over the teal waters of the Pelorus River.

BOTTOM LEFT Evening light on tussocks above Rocks Hut, looking towards Dun Saddle, Pelorus River Track.

BOTTOM RIGHT Picking a way through the rocky bed of Hacket Creek, Richmond Alpine Track.

OPPOSITE Viewed from near Starveall Hut, Mount Rintoul and Purple Top (traversed by the Richmond Alpine Track) catch the last of the evening light.

LEFT Beech forest and tussock cover on the ridge between Mount Starveall and Slaty Peak.

RIGHT Easy tops tramping along the range between Old Man and Little Rintoul.

OPPOSITE A view through beech trees to Old Man Hut and its adjacent tarn, Richmond Alpine Track.

OPPOSITE The trail follows craggy tops over Little Rintoul (Northbound view).

LEFT Mount Rintoul (1,731 m), high point of the trail in the Richmond Ranges and one of the highest points overall, viewed from Little Rintoul.

RIGHT Cairn and warratah on the summit of Mount Rintoul.

Moonlit exposure of Rintoul Hut, one of many regular huts on the route through the Richmond Ranges.

Open silver beech forest, Richmond Alpine Track.

LEFT Wairoa River near Mid Wairoa Hut. Gorged in places, some tough tramping sidles its edge.

RIGHT Forest interior above the Wairoa River, along with a cheeky South Island robin.

LEFT Beech forest near Tarn Hut, Richmond Alpine Track.

RIGHT Top Wairoa Hut sits on the margin between beech forest and the Red Hills ultramafic (mineral-rich, low silica rock) zone.

OPPOSITE Red Hills ultramafic zone from Mount Ellis. This region of igneous and meta-igneous rock is thrust up from 10 km or more below the Earth's crust. The thin tussock and scrub cover is a consequence of soil too toxic for tree growth.

ABOVE A block of coarse ultramafic rock in the Motueka Valley.

ABOVE Red Hills Hut and alpine wetlands at the end of the Richmond Alpine Track.
OPPOSITE Lake Rotoiti, gateway to Nelson Lakes National Park. The trail follows its left edge before entering Travers Valley (centre).

TOP LEFT Travers River and John Tait Hut, Waiau Pass Track, Nelson Lakes National Park.

TOP RIGHT Travers River and mountain beech forest, Travers Valley.

BOTTOM LEFT Section tramper Hana Black pauses beside the Travers River en route to Travers Saddle.

BOTTOM RIGHT Mossy mountain beech forest in the upper Travers Valley.

Upper Travers Hut, cradled in the beautiful alpine cirque of the upper Travers Valley.

LEFT Weaving through ancient moraine and landslide debris near Travers Saddle.
RIGHT Weather closes in over Mount Travers (2,338 m), Travers Saddle.

LEFT Showery weather on the sinuous descent into the East Sabine Valley below Travers Saddle.

RIGHT Rotomairewhenua (the lake of peaceful lands) – more commonly known as Blue Lake – contains the clearest known fresh water in the world.

RIGHT Blue Lake ringed by mountain beech in the upper valley. The lake's clarity comes from the filtration its waters receive as they drain though ancient landslide material from its source, Lake Constance.

Viewed from the landslide material that formed Lake Constance, the tussocky mountainside beyond is the trail's route to the lake head and Waiau Pass.

ABOVE Bad weather begins to obscure the view from the high sidle around Lake Constance toward the lake's head. Waiau Pass is just out of sight up the valley.

OPPOSITE Crossing Waiau Pass (1,870 m) after wet weather deteriorated to a snow storm.

TOP LEFT Mid Waiau Valley and Lake Hill, near Ada Homestead.

BOTTOM LEFT The barren, forest-cleared hills of the mid Waiau Valley and Waiau River, near the Ada River confluence.

RIGHT Lichen on tree branch, St James Walkway.

OPPOSITE Anne Hut and the high, open valley of the Henry River, St James Walkway.

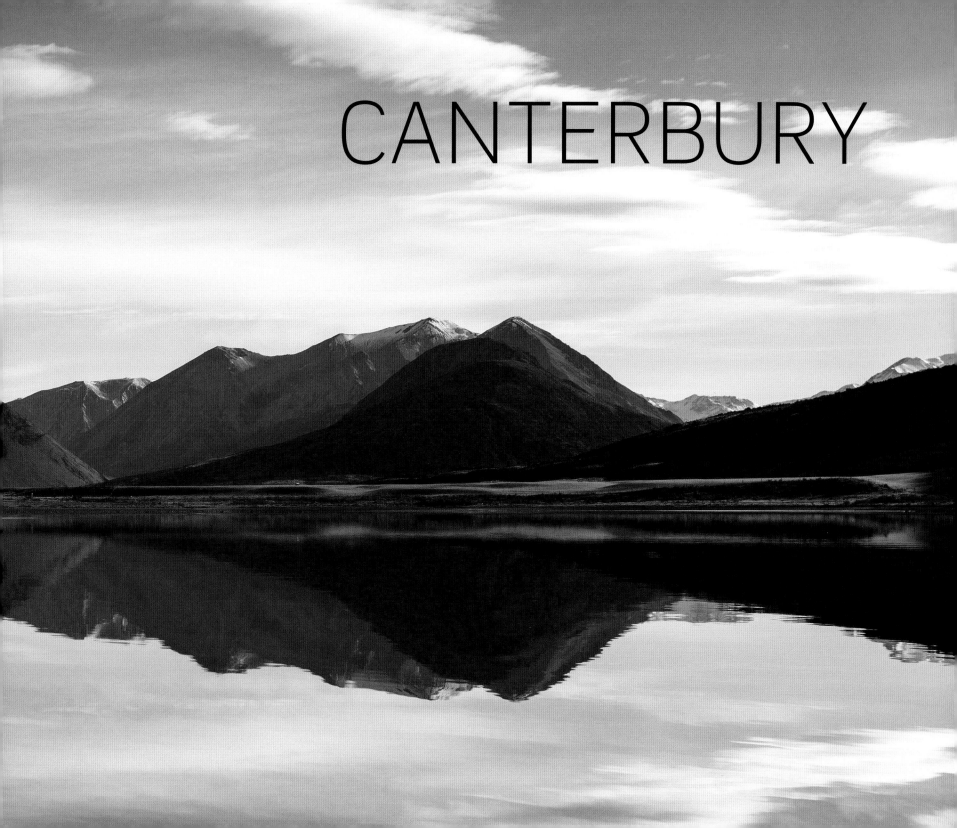

CANTERBURY

CANTERBURY
Boyle River–Ahuriri Valley

*And here was a plant happily suited to plain, hill or mountain – the tussock – of which
neither the earth nor the eye could tire. It seemed to me a plant of the spaces...*
—FROM *SOUTH ISLAND JOURNAL*, T.H. SCOTT [1950]

The silvery braids of big rivers, broad alluvial basins and a landscape softened with tan
alpine grasses are the hallmarks of Canterbury. Mostly lying east of the Main Divide
and often on the high country shoulder of the Southern Alps the Te Araroa Trail through
this region is one of wide-open views, mountain grandeur and a measure of history.

Used as a route by Māori for pounamu (greenstone) trading and by Europeans during
the 1860s gold rush, Harper Pass has long been a passage to the West Coast; its sense of
history made more tangible by a series of historic huts. The open forest and grassy flats
of the Hurunui give way to the rawness of the West Coast dramatically on the west side
of the pass. Ragged gullies, fast streams and knotted bush are typical of the land until
the trail takes you east again into the expanse of the Waimakariri Valley.

The Harper River Track is a final chance to enjoy beech forest before the great glacier-
shaped valleys and wide skies of the central Canterbury foothills. Much of the route
from the Rakaia River to Tekapo is in tussock country once grazed by high country
sheep stations and now in the conservation estate. Many old musterer's huts, some
restored, add considerable character and welcome shelter. Stag Saddle (1,925 m) in the
Two Thumb Range is Te Araroa's highest point and the view of Lake Tekapo and the
Mackenzie Basin will be well earned.

The long walk across the Mackenzie Basin is memorable for the turquoise waters of
Lake Pukaki and the unbroken mountains of the Southern Alps on the horizon. A crossing
of the Ohau Range gives entry to another of the Alps' big drainages, the Ahuriri Valley.

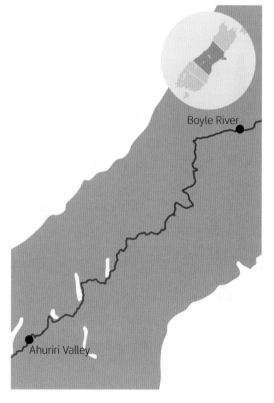

Boyle River

Ahuriri Valley

PREVIOUS PAGES Lake Georgina, Harper Road. Northbound view to Cottons Sheep Range, Round Hill and Mount Ida.

OPPOSITE Overlooking Stag Saddle (1,925 m), high point of the Te Araroa Trail, from Beuzenberg Peak, Two Thumb Range.

TOP LEFT Mellow grasslands lead towards Hope Kiwi Saddle, Hope Kiwi Track.

BOTTOM LEFT View south down the Hurunui River, Harper Pass Track.

RIGHT Beech forest interior on the margin of the open Hurunui Valley, Harper Pass Track.

OPPOSITE The open flats of the Hurunui River near Hurunui No. 3 Hut.

TOP LEFT Interior of the historic Hurunui No. 3 Hut, built in 1939 by the Public Works Department as accommodation for a government-sponsored commercial tramping route over Harper's Pass, a scheme not eventually realised.

TOP RIGHT The author's feet on a three-wire bridge, Harper Pass Track.

BOTTOM LEFT Camerons Hut and open flats. A strong sense of history pervades the Harpers Pass crossing, its valleys long trod by Māori, gold miners and generations of hunters and trampers.

BOTTOM RIGHT The author at Harpers Pass Bivouac, a classic New Zealand Forest Service two-bunk design.

The Hurunui Valley narrows and the river shrinks as Harpers Pass is approached.

OPPOSITE View into the upper Taramakau Valley from shortly below Harpers Pass. Locke Stream Hut is located at the end of the first prominent bush tongue.

LEFT Bush transitions as the trail nears the subalpine zone and Harpers Pass.

TOP RIGHT The bush changes from mixed beech forest on the east side of Harpers Pass to denser and and more varied species on the west.

BOTTOM RIGHT Completed in 1940, historic Locke Stream Hut is one of a series of five huts (including Hurunui No. 3) built by the Public Works Department. The hut's timber was milled by hand nearby, during the depths of winter and construction started the following spring.

TOP LEFT Log and bright lichen covered stones, typical of the wetter western valleys of the Arthur's Pass region, Taramakau Valley.

TOP RIGHT Confluence of the Otehake and Taramakau Rivers. Potentially one of the more serious crossings of Te Araroa, these rivers can delay walkers in times of heavy or prolonged rain.

BOTTOM LEFT Confluence of the Deception and Otira Rivers near State Highway 73. The trail takes the Deception River (left) from here towards Goat Pass, also the course of the demanding Coast to Coast race.

BOTTOM RIGHT The Sanctuary, budget accommodation at Arthur's Pass Village; a short detour from the route of the trail and an essential resupply stop.

OPPOSITE Wide valleys and open landscape east of the Divide: looking from above Lagoon Saddle, Harper River Track, to the Waimakariri Valley and its confluence with the Bealey (photo centre).

The last days of autumn freeze a tarn on Lagoon Saddle, Harper River Track.

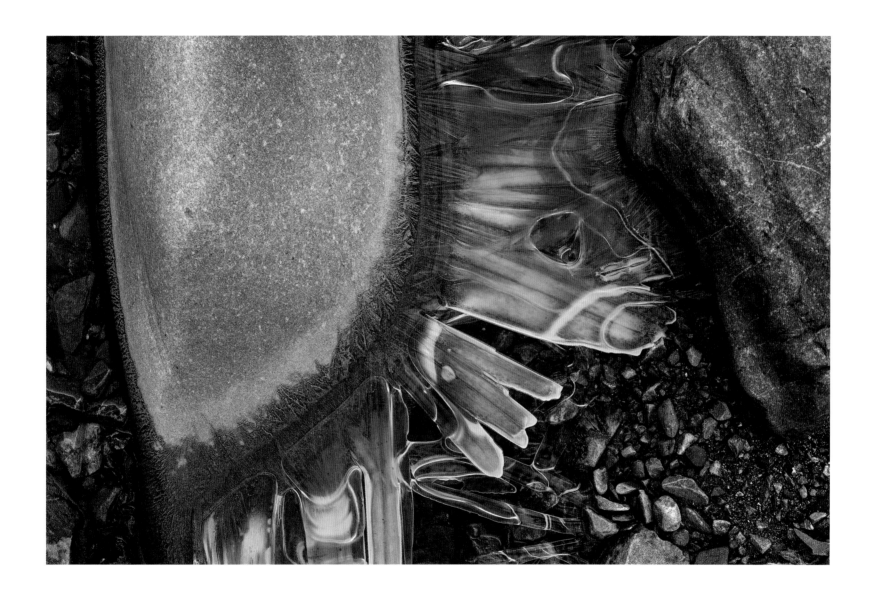

Ice and greywacke forms intriguing shapes in the bed of the Harper River.

OPPOSITE Hamilton Creek and the beech forest-clad Craigieburn Range, near Hamilton Hut, Harper River Track.

LEFT A cold morning in the Harper River after a late autumn snowfall.

RIGHT The Pinnacles, Harper Valley.

TOP LEFT Farm buildings, Lake Coleridge Station, Homestead Road.

TOP RIGHT The Rakaia River valley from Lake Coleridge township. The Rakaia is a trail 'hazard zone' and as such not officially part of the route. The trail re-enters the ranges at Glenrock Stream, behind the spur at photo centre.

BOTTOM LEFT Matagouri, Turtons Saddle. Te Araroa walkers will become familiar with its spiky touch.

BOTTOM RIGHT View down Glenrock Stream to the Rakaia and Wilberforce Valleys.

Comyns Hut and confluence of Turtons and Hakatere Streams below the Black Hill Range, Clent Hills Track.

LEFT Ice clad boulder in Hakatere Stream, Clent Hills Track.

RIGHT Open tussock country on Clent Hills Saddle, looking south west towards the Lake Heron Basin.

OPPOSITE Longman Range and Ricki Spur (centre), Lake Heron Basin. The trail descends here and follows the valley left.

TOP LEFT Relics of a bygone era of high country farming fade on a saddle above Lake Heron Basin.

TOP RIGHT Heron Road, Lake Heron Basin.

BOTTOM LEFT The small settlement of Lake Clearwater and Harper Range from Mount Guy Saddle.

BOTTOM RIGHT Sunrise catches heavy cloud over Mount Guy and Clearwater Track.

North westerly cloud forms over Clearwater Track north of Mount Guy, ahead of rain and higher winds in the mountains.

TOP LEFT A gusting wind picks up dust from the Rangitata River bed.

TOP RIGHT Crooked Spur Hut, Two Thumb Track. One of the many classic and varied musterer's huts that provide rustic accommodation through Canterbury.

BOTTOM LEFT View south from Beuzenberg Peak towards Camp Stream and Lake Tekapo beyond.

BOTTOM RIGHT Tramping the classic 'Snake Ridge', a very worthwhile alternative route to the lower valley from Stag Saddle.

OPPOSITE Stag Saddle, Two Thumb Range. Viewed from Beuzenberg Peak in alpenglow prior to dawn. The route crosses the gentle pass (photo centre) from left to right.

OPPOSITE Tussock hillsides in the lower valley, Camp Stream, Two Thumb Range.

TOP LEFT Dating back to 1898, Camp Stream Hut is a comfortable four bunk ex-musterers' hut, restored and maintained by the Mackenzie Alpine Trust.

BOTTOM LEFT An old roadmans hut on Braemar Road, open for public use and often utilised by Te Araroa walkers.

RIGHT Braemar Road and Ben Ōhau Range on the approach to Lake Pukaki.

Aoraki Mount Cook (3,734 m), flanked by La Perouse (left) and Mount Tasman (right) rises above Lake Pukaki.

Lake Pukaki's colour, a result of glacial flour-laden water, reflected in cloud over the lake and Ben Ōhau Range.

TOP LEFT Salmon farming is a big local industry for the Mackenzie Basin, Lake Ruataniwha, Twizel.

TOP RIGHT Willow tree on the shore of Lake Ōhau. Ben Ōhau peak catches the last of the evening sun.

BOTTOM LEFT Lenticular clouds over Lake Ōhau indicate impending stormy weather for the alps.

BOTTOM RIGHT Tussock and scree country in the East Branch of the Ahuriri River, Te Araroa's route over the Ōhau Range.

OPPOSITE A north westerly storm builds over ranges alongside the Ahuriri Valley.

OTAGO

OTAGO
Ahuriri Valley–North Mavora Lake

We were hunters and foragers. The frontier was everywhere. We were bounded only by the earth, and the ocean, and the sky. The open road still softly calls...
—CARL SAGAN

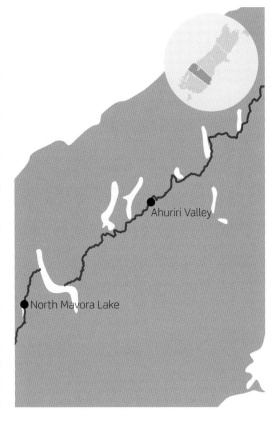

Metamorphosed – forged inside the Earth – uplifted and eroded by water, wind and the ravages of glaciers, the Otago landscape is distinctive. Its schists giving an origami-like angularity to the landscape. Great lakes fill the basins left by ice that is now confined to higher mountains, including Otago's iconic centrepiece – Mount Aspiring; visible from Breast Hill if you're there on a clear day.

Essentially a series of three classic tramping trips, two followed by big towns and easy walking 'connections', Otago adds another dimension to the Te Araroa experience. Hāwea Conservation Park, via the Avon Burn, gives entry to Otago's first ranges. These mountains, long ago cleared of bush, are etched by pioneers' bulldozer tracks, sometimes seen crossing the most unlikely of ridges and faces, and the trail follows them intermittently to Lake Hāwea. The deep vee of the Timaru Valley invokes a sense of remoteness; the tramping is tough here but the broad heights and big views of Breast Hill – one of the trail's memorable moments – follow.

Mellow flats and lake-edge walking through the Wanaka region provides a break for the legs before the sinuous ridges of the Motatapu Alpine Track. This tough pass-hopping delight – its wind-battered fences a testament to the tenacity of high country farmers – gives entry to the historic gold settlement of Macetown, followed by quaint Arrowtown. Enjoy the luxury offered by the Wakatipu basin resort towns while it lasts, as more remoteness follows with the Mavora Walkway. Abundant beech forest, the first since North Canterbury, cloaks the land in green through to the Mararoa River where the country turns to tussock again. Past Careys Hut the valley fills with a placid blue; North Mavora Lake heralding the start of Southland.

PREVIOUS PAGES Lake Wakatipu, Mount Bonpland (2,343 m) and the entrance to Greenstone Valley at left, Te Araroa's route onwards through the mountain valleys of Otago.
OPPOSITE The main street of Arrowtown maintains plenty of charm, thanks to its gold mining legacy.

TOP LEFT Tin Hut, a private musterer's hut in the Avon Burn, en route to Mount Martha Saddle.

TOP RIGHT Timaru River, below Top Timaru Hut, in flood after heavy rain.

BOTTOM LEFT The Timaru River is crossed a dozen times as it's followed downstream towards the Stodys Hut junction.

BOTTOM RIGHT Snow shower in the Timaru Valley.

Northbound view of the Timaru Valley after a fresh early June snowfall.

LEFT View south over Otago's broad schist ranges from Breast Hill Track.

RIGHT The route from the Avon Burn to Lake Hāwea follows old bulldozer tracks intermittently, this one leading along the tussocky tops towards Breast Hill.

LEFT Evening light over the Lower Timaru Valley and Hāwea Conservation Park ranges from Breast Hill Track.

RIGHT A muted winter dawn over the steep escarpment of Breast Hill.

OPPOSITE Gwilym Griffith-Jones checks out the view from Breast Hill Track towards Lake Hāwea and township. A long and spectacular ridge descent to reach the flat follows.

LEFT Views of Lake Hāwea and steep ridges parallel the descent to the lake, one of the highlights of Te Araroa.

TOP RIGHT The oft-photographed 'Wanaka Tree'; a lonely willow, its branches laden with nesting cormorants.

BOTTOM RIGHT Lake Wanaka at Wanaka township, crystal clear on a crisp winter's morning.

Schist boulders and Lake Wanaka in the alpenglow of a Central Otago evening. Glendhu Bay Track.

TOP LEFT Dramatic ridge tramping among the steep hills of the Motatapu Track. Knuckle Peak in the background.

TOP RIGHT Highland Creek Hut, one of three comfortable overnight stops on the Motatapu Alpine Track.

BOTTOM LEFT Muted dawn light gently illuminates ridges and ranges above the Motatapu Valley.

BOTTOM RIGHT Streambeds dissect the floor of the Motatapu Valley, below the route's descent from the edge of Knuckle Peak (northbound view).

TOP LEFT Camping in Arrow Valley after a snowstorm, Motatapu Alpine Track.

BOTTOM LEFT Crossing Arrow River before sunrise. From here the usual route follows the river downstream for several kilometres; a significantly more pleasant walk during the warmth of a summer's day.

RIGHT The Remarkables and Lake Hayes make an impressive backdrop while descending the Big Hill Walkway towards Arrowtown.

A tourist-laden jet boat passes beneath the historic Shotover Bridge, Shotover River. The Remarkables dominant in the background.

Te Araroa provides a gentle entry to the bustling tourist town of Queenstown along the edge of Lake Wakatipu.

LEFT The Greenstone River passes through a narrow cleft below Greenstone Hut.

TOP RIGHT Beech forest, Pass Burn, Mavora Wakway.

BOTTOM RIGHT Ice encapsulated beech seedlings, Mavora Walkway.

LEFT Boundary Hut, Mavora Walkway, beneath the Milky Way, with the faint glow of Aurora Australis on the distant horizon.

TOP RIGHT A curious South Island robin keeps the photographer company at North Mavora Lake.

BOTTOM RIGHT Beech trees frame a peak in the Livingston Mountains, Mavora Walkway.

Careys Hut and North Mavora Lake in the calm of a winter morning.

SOUTHLAND

SOUTHLAND
North Mavora Lake–Bluff

Contrary to how it may feel while you're hiking, the trail does not end at a magical portal through which you transcend arbitrary existence and become one with the great wide everything. Instead it ends at about where you started, except now you can't stop crying and you're too broke to pay the rent…
—CARROT QUINN, AUTHOR OF *THRU-HIKING WILL BREAK YOUR HEART*

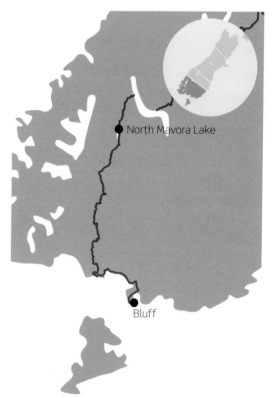

North Mavora Lake

Bluff

The coastal boundaries of New Zealand give Te Araroa natural beginning and end points. While the sea is an occasional companion walking the North Island, completing the trek at Bluff the trail has not seen land's edge since Marlborough. Not only do the trail's origin and terminus share dramatic coastlines, but the regions also have in common a frontier ruggedness. Between islands of bush and tussock covered downs, Te Araroa heads through farmland and enters no large townships until Riverton, on the coast.

Bolstered by the Mavora Lakes, the Mararoa River flows south and Te Araroa flanks it through bush and along river terraces. From the braids of the lower river the Takitimu Mountains stand in the distance. This range is one of the first on the South Island to catch the weather and has a reputation for wild winds. The country here makes for a beautiful tramp through pockets of beech – wispy with lichen and softened by moss.

The Longwood Range follows, and as you tread its crown of subalpine scrub you're walking the last high ground of the trail. The great arc of beach between Riverton and Invercargill curls away, capped by Bluff Hill and the end of the walk. Descending to the coast the trail follows history once again, taking the path of a 19th century water race, once used to sluice gold from nearby hills.

Te Araroa returns to the coast at Colac Bay, coming almost full circle, walking once again with the silence of the dunes and the churning of the surf. Riverton and New Zealand's most southern city provide pause before the final leg to Bluff, culminating at Stirling Point via the Foveaux Walkway – a beautiful and exposed headland with views of Stewart Island/Rakiura.

PREVIOUS PAGES The final high ground of Te Araroa's journey south, the southern Longwood Range gives a view to Riverton's harbour, and Bluff Hill, beyond.
OPPOSITE Mountain flax/wharariki and boulders of igneous rock on the broad top of Bald Hill, Longwood Range. Looking north toward the Takitimu Mountains.

TOP LEFT Heavy frost licks the surface of a frozen beach, South Mavora Lake.

TOP RIGHT Walk bridge across the South Mavora Lake outlet, Mararoa River Track. The open silver beech forest a constant companion for the walk along the lake and down valley.

BOTTOM LEFT View north west along the Mararoa River to Snowdon Forest. The trail here follows an indistinct path along the river margin.

BOTTOM RIGHT The Takitimu Mountains, snow capped in winter, from the open flats of the mid Mararoa Valley.

OPPOSITE Mavora Lakes Road (northbound view).

LEFT Track junction below Bog Burn Saddle, Takitimu Mountains.

RIGHT Ground trail beside the Spence Burn, near Aparima Hut.

OPPOSITE Waterloo Burn, Takitimu Mountains. Alternating travel through beech forest and tussock downs is characteristic of tramping in the Takitimus.

LEFT Beech forest and fern-rich ground cover, Takitimu Mountains.

TOP RIGHT Moss clad, beech forest interior, Wairaki Valley.

BOTTOM RIGHT The Telford Burn running big after frequent rain. This river is the walker's exit from the Takitimu Range, prior to crossing Mount Linton Station (northbound view).

The Takitimu Mountains and Te Araroa's farm road route across Mount Linton Station.

OPPOSITE The Takitimu Mountains and rolling pasture, lush from a wet winter, viewed from Twinlaw.

TOP LEFT Private farm building, Birchwood.

TOP RIGHT Sheep graze their winter feed before a backdrop of the Takitimu Mountains.

BOTTOM LEFT Road junction, Scotts Gap Feldwick Road.

BOTTOM RIGHT Fresh snowfall on beech forest, Longwood Range.

TOP LEFT Beautiful open flax and tussock country and occasional boulders on the walk along the crown of the Longwood Range.

BOTTOM LEFT Regenerating silver beech forest alongside Ports Water Race.

RIGHT Gold stamping battery, Ports Water Race. A relic of the gold mining era that brought hundreds of Chinese immigrants to the region.

Crossing headlands during stormy south westerly weather, Tihaka Beach Track.

TOP LEFT The harbour at Jacobs River Estuary, Riverton.

TOP RIGHT Driftwood and snowy sand dunes, Oreti Beach.

BOTTOM LEFT Finishing almost as it starts, Te Araroa takes to a long stretch of beach once again for the Oreti Beach Track into Invercargill.

BOTTOM RIGHT Troopers Memorial, Invercargill. Te Araroa's final city stop before its conclusion at Bluff.

An abandoned and wrecked vessel on the outskirts of Bluff.

LEFT An outcrop of norite (plutonic rock) on Bluff Hill/Motupōhue, Foveaux Walkway.

RIGHT Buildings alongside State Highway One, Bluff.

OPPOSITE Wind-swept and wave-washed, Stirling Point is the southern terminus of State Highway One and the Te Araroa Trail.

TRAIL NOTES
Walking and photographing New Zealand's Trail

Are you looking for the perfect shot?
—AN AHIPARA LOCAL

Long distance tramping distills life to simple pleasures and perceptions: the warmth of the rising sun on the side of your face; the cool touch of mist on the wind; the luxurious sensation of dry feet and fresh socks. You fall into tune with your surroundings, your hearing on alert. The cluck and scratch of pukekos in a paddock, the tick-tack of walking poles, the crunch of your shoes on gravel or the squelch of beechy loam become the soundscape to your experience.

I am an advocate of the through-tramp approach to accomplishing Te Araroa. Any long-distance journey, especially self-powered, is by its very nature an immersive experience. One is consumed by the task at hand, the daily routines, the rewards, the perpetual obsession with food and the enriching sensation of intense daily exercise. Nothing else replicates this, and it's when you set yourself free to embark on such adventures that the greatest rewards and insights – both into yourself, and the world – are manifest.

I walked the trail north to south, starting on 18th January and finishing on 8th July on a wet and windy Southland day. My total time was 171 days, comprising 154 walking days, 17 rest/logistic/administration days and several half days where I did illogical distances to be well situated for photography. Te Araroa through-trampers doing both islands typically start earlier; I began walking about six weeks later than usual. It would mean a mid-winter finish, but this gave me three seasons to walk through and a greater range of conditions to photograph. I also enjoyed the peace of the trail at this time, usually having the huts to myself. Vermin, often a problem in summer, were scarce and sandflies

few. The shorter days, heavier equipment, cold temperatures and snow of winter provided a greater physical challenge, but this bolstered my experience of the trail.

All walkers are constrained at times by the weather, this is by far the biggest external influence over any trail experience. Storms flood New Zealand's rivers – and snow can fall on the ranges – at any time of the year. I was lucky to have difficult snow conditions on only two mountain passes but rivers halted my progress, or made it more difficult, several times.

New Zealand is a country of weather extremes, situated as it is in the notorious latitudes of the windy Roaring Forties. With a relatively warm ocean to the west and Antarctica to the south, the air masses over New Zealand are changeable. By example; in the Mackenzie Basin in early June the mercury in my thermometer showed a low of minus 7 degrees one morning, then plus 10 degrees the next, ahead of a warm and wet north-westerly storm moving onto the country. Snowfalls to low elevations in late May and early June left some of Te Araroa's South Island passes under a half a metre of snow, with sustained cooler temperatures following these falls, keeping the snow in place. However a very warm and wet storm in the second week of June obliterated much of this snow within 36 hours, flooding rivers and delaying me in the Timaru Valley while I waited for the river to drop.

Being outside for such a sustained period of time increases your awareness of an essential photographic ingredient: light. Being free to observe its changes and subtleties was a luxury of the Te Araroa experience, and photographer or not, it is worth starting early to witness the ephemeral light of a new day reveal the land before you. Some moments felt serendipitous, when a particular quality of light or a coincidence strengthened an image, but I could only imagine what I might have missed when conditions did not click or I was simply not at a place at the best time of the day to shoot. A limitation of this project was that I generally only had a single opportunity at any given location, so had to utilise subject and light to try to reveal a location's character with the conditions at hand. I returned to only two locations after the walk, to shoot extra images in Wellington and Queenstown.

I carried a Canon EOS 5D MKII camera, with four lenses: 16-35mm f2.8, 50mm f1.2, 70-200mm f4 and a 24mm tilt shift lens. Along with filters, batteries, accessories and tripod this amounted to nearly eight kilograms in addition to regular trail walking equipment. To offset the load of my photography gear I opted for ultra-light tramping equipment. Bivouac Outdoor generously provided me with a range of products. I carried little in the way of clothing from Cape Reinga, but added and swapped clothing as required as temperatures dropped. I used three different sleeping bags over the course of the walk and three different types of boots, to suit the vastly differing climate and terrain.

With the increasing popularity of long distance hiking, there is a trend to take weight savings to extremes. It makes sense to choose equipment carefully, purging non-essentials, but a slightly heavier pack will not ruin your long distance experience. I was concerned about the weight of my pack at the start of the walk, but I adapted to the extra weight quickly and would not say that my heavier load detracted from my walk – if anything I feel a greater satisfaction from having accomplished it with what – by modern trail standards – was an unfeasible load.

While the photography in this book concentrates on the landscapes of Te Araroa, the trail is also strongly a 'people' experience. In the North Island in particular, I observed an inherent curiosity towards trail walkers. Social barriers apparently dissolve when you put on a pack and walk rural roads and urban areas – it makes you approachable. I was asked many questions by complete strangers but I found myself just as likely to start a conversation with passers by, in part to connect with a place on a deeper level but also as a reaction to long periods of solitude. The statement 'I'm walking the length of New Zealand' was often met with incredulity by people who would then ask 'but where have you left the car?' as if I were using one for transitions between tramps.

The road-walking element of the Te Araroa Trail is an acquired taste. Approximately 13 per cent of the trail is currently on road margin, mostly rural road. Some trail walkers actively dislike it – preferring to hitch-hike, while others accept it with an open mind. I relished the opportunity to experience whatever novelty the day or landscape might provide – be it by road or trail. The road is as much a part of the story of New Zealand as the hills and often I found the easy walking of the road sections left my mind free to ruminate on the context and variety of the walk.

A sensation I missed after the walk was the anticipation for food after a few days in the hills. The sheer pleasure of having that hunger sated on arrival in a town: steak, vegetables, bakery treats and beer were always high on the list. Walking eight to twelve hours a day over nearly six months resulted in the loss of about five kilograms in body weight. The loss accelerated in the South Island, due to light rations and long days, and I had to bolster my diet in an effort to thwart the cold.

Long distance journeys are a mental game. There's discomfort. There are days that feel hard. But there are also days where the kilometres fly by, when you feel light on your feet – free and fast among the landscape. It takes patience to accept the bad days with the good and it is important to remember that strength comes with time. Physical training might ready you for walking but building the right frame of mind to deal with the ups and downs – both physical and metaphorical – is more difficult. Determination is your biggest asset.

ACKNOWLEDGEMENTS

A tramp the length of the country cannot be accomplished without the help of others. A great many people assisted me along the way: strangers with whom I had meaningful conversations after stopping to ask for water, trail angels, old friends and family. An unanticipated benefit of the walk was the opportunity it provided to reconnect with people – scattered by the diaspora of life – some of whom I had not seen for many years.

My partner Hana's commitment to this project has been as great as mine, her logistical support, food parcels, company and patience kept the wheels on the wagon.

I'd like to thank: Sarah Adcock, Bridgid Allan and Ant Peacocke, Marcus Bai, Bill at The Sanctuary, Russell and Noeline Black, Elissa Brittenden and Grant Singleton, Rob Brown, Chris Burtenshaw, Andrew Caldwell, Chapman family, Guillaume Charton and Aurelia Margot, Mariata Couch and John Paki, Vicky Danrell, Di Drayton, Katie Dunlop, Ngaire Dunn, Sally Duxfield and Makahika Outdoor Pursuits Centre, Gwilym Griffith-Jones and Merle Schlüter, Matt Evans and Femme Kloss, Kristen Foley, Steve Fortune, Ruth and Jeremy Heath, Holger Horner, Lynda Jackson at Land's End, Peter Karam, Arch King of Air Rangitata, Berwyn Jenkins and Lot 3 cafe, Chris Maclean, Simon Middlemass and Pip Walter, Mount Potts Lodge, Janelle Palmer, Lisa Peacock, Tom Riley and Anna Pilbrow, Rachel Sanson and Scott Burnett, Barry Savage, Andrew Smith and Kaf Henderson, Sarah Smith, Miriama Tukere (Turangawaewae Marae), Helen Kotua (Turangawaewae House), Rachael Mayne, Colin Monteath, Michelle and Tim Robinson, Kate Schimanski, Tania and Wayne Simpson, Polly Stupples, Sutherland family, Joseph Treanor, Bevan Triebels, Julia Valigore, Ivan Vostinar and Simone Higgie, Janelle and Martin Wallace, John Watson and Sandy McInnes and especially Pete Griffin who gave valuable opinions on both images and words. A few people in this list also shared the walk with me, whether a short urban stretch, or a week in the wilds. You know who you are – thanks for the company and conversation.

I'm grateful to New Holland Publishers, especially Christine Thomson, for being receptive to a bold idea and for her guidance that has allowed this book to morph from a general concept into the product that it has become. Credit also goes to designer Thomas Casey for the book's presentation and for his balanced view and sense of priority that has helped refine the book's images. Thanks also to Carrot Quinn, Otago University Press and Joan Dutton who gave permission to reprint poetry and quotes. Federated Mountain Clubs showed strong support for this project with a generous grant from their Mountain and Forest Trust.

Trail pioneer Geoff Chapple supplied a fitting foreword and I thank him, Te Araroa Trust and the many volunteers who have made New Zealand's Trail possible. The trail will be valued and appreciated by generations to come.

I was fortunate to have supportive sponsors supply equipment and food for my walk. Thank you to: Bivouac Outdoor, Kathmandu/Salomon, Absolute Wilderness, Hubbards, Nice & Natural, Oasis Beauty, Lacklands/Sandisk, SealLine & Bridgedale, courtesy of Ampro.